CW01333065

Foreword

James Gibson
A Tribute from Alex Ferguson
Manager, Manchester United

Where would Manchester United be today without James Gibson?

Chances are that the Club, which now stands amongst the elite in the world of football, would probably be a distant memory.

True benefactors in the Gibson mould are a rare commodity and it's nice to see his story being told in full at long last.

I think I'm right in saying that the Club was twice in sight of being dissolved. It first found itself in financial difficulty in 1902 when the Club changed its name from Newton Heath to Manchester United. It was a man called John Henry Davis, a brewer, and several business colleagues who came to the rescue with funds that allowed the Club to continue.

The Club weathered that storm and went on to become one of the powers in the game during the pre-First World War period.

However, the period between the two World Wars saw United struggling once again and in the early 1930s they had drifted again into troubled waters and that's when James Gibson, a clothing manufacturer in North Manchester, came to the aid of the Club.

His enthusiasm and generosity when United needed it most can never be overstated and I'm sure if he were with us today he would be very proud of the Club he saved.

I was delighted when asked to provide a few words for this very commendable publication which tells the story of an unsung hero in the colourful and fascinating history of Manchester United.

Best Wishes
Alex Ferguson

Alex Ferguson

Dedication

This book is dedicated to James Gibson, the Chairman and President of Manchester United 1931 - 1951. His passion for the Club shone like a beacon - his inspiration and energy must never be forgotten.

The research, writing and publishing of this book would not have been possible without the help of many people.

Particular credit must go to members of James Gibson's family. The vision of Alan and Frances Embling provided the catalyst for this publication; their unwavering support and enthusiasm throughout the project made it happen.

Many other people contributed to the work. Their continuous help was very much appreciated and without them the book would never have been completed. Thanks go to:

Acknowledgements

Alan Gibson
Andrew Embling
Annemarie Wright

Betty Bidwell	Alan Graver
Charlie Mitten	Yannick Monteyne
Jimmy Diggle	Mark Havercroft
Jim Moore	Susan Booth
Alex Ferguson	David Sadler
Cliff Butler	Ken Merrett
Andrew Edwards	Brian Walker
Sandy Busby	Paul Gravett
Vera Fell	Mark Bryant
Christopher Butterworth	David Allison

The original cartoons within this book are owned by Alan and Frances Embling. Rather than let the cartoons remain hidden from public view it is their expressed wish that these remarkable pictures are available for everyone to see.

The Gibson Guarantee

This cartoon is the first picture of the series in this book. It depicts James Gibson, as Prince Charming, saving Manchester United from bankruptcy in 1931. In his hand is 'The Gibson Guarantee' - the money that gave the Club a future.

There is one elementary Truth - ignorance of which kills countless ideas and splendid plans:
The moment one definitely commits oneself, then providence moves too.
Whatever you can do, or dream you can do. Begin it.
Boldness has genius, power and magic in it. Begin it now.

Johann Wolfgang von Goethe (1749-1832)

Appendix 1

1)	Manchester Evening News	Saturday December 19	1931
(2)	How a Club was Saved (Stacey Lintott)		1956
(3)	Manchester Guardian	Tuesday December 22	1931
(4)	Manchester Evening News	Monday December 21	1931
(5)	Manchester Evening News	Thursday January 7	1932
(6)	Manchester Evening News	Thursday July 14	1932
(7)	Manchester Evening News	Saturday October 1	1932
(8)	Manchester United The History of a Great Football Club - Percy M Young Page 114. Heinemann		1960
(9)	The Daily Mail	Monday May 4	1936
(10)	Manchester Guardian	November 10	1937
(11)	Manchester Evening News	Monday October 4	1937
(12)	Manchester Evening News	Friday October 22	1937
(13)	Manchester United The History of a Great Football Club - Percy M Young Page 130. Heinemann		1960
(14)	Manchester Evening News	Wednesday January 28	1948
(15)	Manchester United The History of a Great Football Club - Percy M Young Page 143. Heinemann		1960

Introduction

Many books have been written about Manchester United's history and the personalities that have played their part in making it one of the world's greatest football Clubs.

From humble beginnings in 1878 when a group of men from the Lancashire and Yorkshire Railway Company decided to start their own football team, Newton Heath, to the winning of a magnificent League and Cup double in 1994, much has happened.

Victories in the League, FA and European Cups, the tragedy of Munich and the glory that Sir Matt Busby brought to the Club have all been well documented. But football at Manchester United during the thirties and forties has a colourful history all of its own. For the first time it is possible to tell the story in detail of how the Club was saved from bankruptcy and how it progressed to become one of the great post-war teams.

Much of the material used in this book has been sourced from books and cuttings owned by the Gibson family. Alan Gibson, the current Vice President of Manchester United joined the Club as a director soon after the War. For over thirty years he acted as a great `ambassador' to the Club, touring with the players wherever they travelled throughout the world.

But it is James William Gibson, Alan Gibson's father, who is the focus of this book. He is the man who first saved the Club from bankruptcy in 1931 and then over a period of twenty years helped rebuild Manchester United and lead it back into the limelight and to the kind of success the Club enjoys today.

The early life of James Gibson

James Gibson was born on October 21 1877, only one year before the Lancashire and Yorkshire Railway Company created Newton Heath. His parents owned a house very close to the centre of Manchester and it was from here that he was brought up with his younger brother, John, and for a short while his sister Florence, who died at an early age.

His father had spent many years developing a successful uniform manufacturing company in the heart of Manchester. Not surprisingly, this type of business flourished in the city, alongside many others which were able to benefit from the fast-changing industrial practices and abundance of textile mills in the region. As a result, the family became accustomed to a high standard of living, and James Gibson was offered his first insight into the practices of running a successful business. However, tragedy struck the Gibson family when James was only a young boy of 14. James' mother and father both contracted fatal illnesses, and the children's lives were thrown into turmoil.

As the eldest son, James grew up quickly. Needing to be strong, he instinctively became a father-figure to his younger brother and sister. Fortunately for the three children they were able to go and live with their Gibson grandparents for a short while and regain some family stability. Unfortunately, further misery soon followed.

Both grandparents died just as the children were adjusting to their new lives. Again, James took charge and became the parental figure for his brother, but it was obvious that the children couldn't fend for themselves. However, it was from this sad and unhappy position that James Gibson's life took one of its most significant twists.

A benevolent uncle, William Fell their mother's only brother, accepted responsibility for James and John and took them all into his care. Like James's father, William Fell was a successful businessman too. Working from the outskirts of Manchester William had become a well-known corn merchant and because of his position he was able to offer James regular employment in virtually all aspects of the business. The young man thrived on the experience and learnt quickly from the opportunity that his uncle had given him. For his part, William immediately recognised the strong qualities in James and within a short space of time the two people developed a deep respect for each other. The responsibility for the children's education and welfare fell to William's two aunts, Rachel and Hannah. Just like the experience of work at the corn merchants, their guidance, generosity and sense of fairness had a marked effect on James's life.

Over the next fifteen years James Gibson enjoyed responsibility in all areas of the work-place. He thrived on hard work and learning new skills. But it was in sales that he excelled and made best use of his talents. Confident in the knowledge of his own ability James began to consider how he might perform if he was working for himself. And it was shortly after the turn of the century that he made the decision to go it alone and set himself up in the business.

The strength of the textile industry in Lancashire at that time was still providing many opportunities for bright entrepreneurs. James Gibson believed that he could create a much wider demand for the use of uniforms and he invested money in a small factory near to the centre of Manchester. Although his father had died over fifteen years ago the Gibson name was still well known in the city and James was able to develop a network of useful contacts quickly. The business grew steadily but it was the onset of the Great War that gave the business its first major break. For the duration of the whole conflict uniforms were manufactured day in day out and by the end of the War in 1918 James Gibson had established himself as a highly successful and respected business man.

However, the demobbing of tens of thousands of men meant that a fresh market had to be found in order to maintain production levels and provide further labour for the workforce. Thinking big, James Gibson proceeded to sell city corporations the idea that tram drivers and conductors would be proud to wear their own uniforms.

Success followed success and by 1924 James Gibson had started to diversify and had set up a number of smaller businesses in areas outside clothing and uniforms. But in this year he also expanded his uniform business by teaming up with Mr F Jones and Mr R H H Briggs to form Briggs, Jones and Gibson. Based in larger premises in Lostock Street, Oldham Road, Manchester, the company was well positioned for further expansion. The partnership between the three men brought together specialist skills and more importantly the capability to sell uniforms to other city corporations further afield.

However, a couple of years after the merger Mr Jones died. This cruel blow to the partnership also came at a time of economic decline and the great depression of the late twenties. The business came under pressure and although his exact reasons are not known (it is thought to be age) Mr Briggs decided to sell his share of the business also. James Gibson bought all the remaining shares and immediately took full control of Briggs, Jones and Gibson. Fortunately, because of his dealings in other areas of business James was able to withstand the slump in trade.

James Gibson and his wife launch the new 'Manchester United' train.

Gibson Family Life

Although James Gibson spent much of his time developing his businesses, he was a strong family man who was very devoted to his wife.

Just after the turn of the century he married Annie Lillian Ward. She had been engaged to another man when she met James but it only took a short while for the couple to realise that they had much in common. Annie Lillian, known as Lillian, was a strong woman who had also been adopted as a young child when her parents died. As a result of this she too had become hardened to the ways of the world - it is perhaps a testament to her wilful character that she insisted that if James wanted to marry her he had to change his faith.

When they married, James Gibson was already a fairly wealthy man. The newly-wedded couple were keen to make their new house a home and create a family to share their happiness with.

Tragically, their first two children (twins) both died at birth and the affect on Annie placed a great stress on her life particularly with James away working so much. Although James Gibson was a successful businessman he loved his home life and the privacy it offered both him and Lillian. His devotion to her and the strength that both had derived from their own difficult childhoods undoubtedly helped the couple get through a extremely painful time.

Not long before the Great War they moved to a house called `The Gables' Dane Road, Sale where a son was born (Norman); although he was very weak he survived birth and it seemed that at last the Gibson family had a child. But following a long and cruel illness, Norman eventually died of pneumonia at the tender age of three.

James and Lillian's final attempts to start a family in 1915 resulted in the premature birth of triplets; again death ravaged the family. Two of the babies died. The one son who managed to survive only did so with the aid of cotton wool wrapping and constant nursing attention over a six month period. This fragile human being was later christened James Alan Gibson.

Lillian Gibson
E.H. MOONEY 1932

As a young boy Alan Gibson's health was never good; his weak chest and the threat of pneumonia made ordinary life almost impossible. He was cared for constantly by his mother and staff who worked in the Gibson house. Even school proved impossible.

Jimmy Diggle who was to prove to be a great friend to Alan remembers him attending a small local private school, Wadham House. However, although Jimmy was to stay at the school until the age of twelve, Alan only stayed for a few days. In fact, Alan's education was conducted mainly at home for fear of his ill health getting the better of him.

But Jimmy continued to visit Alan at home and recalls how James Gibson was very pleasant towards him. "But Mrs Gibson was in charge, she was a pretty tough lady," he said remembering life in the mid twenties.

By this time the Gibson family had moved house again to the place that was to be James Gibson's last home. James and Lillian named the house `Alanor' (after Alan and Norman) and it was to prove to be a magnificent residence for the family for nearly thirty years.

'Alanor' - Home to the Gibson family

James Gibson Saves Manchester United

By 1931 James William Gibson had become an established and well-known businessman in Manchester. He was 53 years old, happily married and his only son, Alan, was beginning to show signs of making a full recovery from illness that had dogged him throughout his childhood.

However, the good fortune of the Gibsons at that time contrasted directly with the situation faced by Manchester United. In the 1930-31 season the club had lost their first twelve league matches causing much disquiet not just within the Club but understandably also amongst supporters.

Following the 5-1 defeat at West Ham on October 11 1930, supporters decided to meet the following Friday to resolve a vote of no confidence in the board of management and to organise a boycott of the Club at the next home match against Arsenal. The secretary of the Manchester United's Supporter's Club, Mr G. Greenhough, was chiefly responsible for organising the meeting which attracted nearly 3000 people.

However, the depth of concern amongst this hard core did not spread to the rest of supporters and the boycott was unsuccessful. Nevertheless, unease remained at the Club and at the end of the season Manchester United finished bottom of the first division having conceded a record 115 goals and losing 27 of their league matches.

The manager, Herbert Bamlett, was sacked in April 1931 and the Club's secretary, Walter Crickmer, was asked to fill the role on a temporary basis, aided by the loyal and charismatic Louis Rocca. At the end of the season the books revealed a loss of £2,509 and a reduction in receipts on first team matches of £7,601. The Manchester Evening News would later disclose that:

"At the end of the 1930/31 season United's financial position was so acute that the Club was unable to guarantee the players' wages during the summer months. (1)

The board of management at Manchester United were left with one ally - hope. Hope that results would improve and that crowds would return in higher numbers to support the Club. However, United were now playing Second Division football and there was little if no money in the pot to buy new players.

The 1931/32 Season

The 1931/32 season started bleakly. Only 3,507 devoted fans passed through the Old Trafford turnstiles to witness the 3-2 defeat against Southampton on September 2. Worse was to come. United only managed to secure 16 points from their first 20 games culminating in a 1-0 home defeat against Bristol City on Saturday 19 December.

But despite this poor result, the day in question would be remembered more for events off the field rather than on it. Behind the scenes wheels were in motion for a change of management and a vital injection of capital at Manchester United. And it was on Saturday 19 December that the Manchester Evening News led with headlines telling readers of how a local business-man was willing to rescue the Club from its perilous position.

"Mr J. W. Gibson, a Manchester business-man with no previous record in big football, has taken over Manchester United for a month, and he has paid the players' wages for this week. He has undertaken to be responsible for the Club's expenditure from December 16 until January 9. If during that time sufficient support is forthcoming at Old Trafford then he is prepared to consider securing a new manager, four first-class players, and the construction of covered accommodation on the popular side of the ground." (1)

In fact, Gibson family artefacts reveal that enough money was made available for all officials and players for a month. Furthermore, James Gibson insisted on maintaining a Club tradition and insisted on buying a Christmas turkey for all the staff on the books.

Nevertheless, the dramatic revelations made public for the first time the extent of the problems at United. Even James Gibson said that he was `amazed' to find the Club in such difficulties and on the brink of bankruptcy. He had always believed Manchester United to be wealthy and yet he found a crippled Club unable to fulfil its remaining fixtures and resigning from the Football League. (2)

James Gibson also discovered that the interest payments on the mortgage with the Brewery Company had lapsed (by agreement) and that payments to creditors like the Stretford Urban District Council were being paid in instalments. Cashflow at the Club had become critical and eventually the bank was forced to withdraw credit facilities.

Bankruptcy at United

It was Walter Crickmer, the temporary manager who brought back the fateful news to the Club that the National Provincial Bank in Spring Gardens, Manchester, was unprepared to offer further credit facilities. The board of management had reached the end but there was still a belief amongst some that Manchester people would support two clubs and that emergency action could still save United.

Although sources differ as to the person responsible for making the approach to James Gibson, it is clear that he agreed immediately and without question to place £2000:00 at the Club's disposal to cover the wage payments. Stacey Lintott, a leading football journalist for 30 years before the war was to write about his view of events twenty five years later.

"The news [that Manchester United was going bankrupt] was a terrific shock. Could nothing be done, I wondered. Suddenly I had a brainwave. For some time I had been lunching with a party that included a Mr James Gibson.

"I knew him to be a successful business-man with a `weakness' for taking over failing businesses and restoring them to solvency. Here was his big chance. He knew nothing of football, had no interest in the game, but that was not necessarily an obstacle. He also had a love of Manchester, and would deeply regret the collapse of such a famous institution as United." (2)

James Gibson's son, Alan, confirms that Stanley Lintott did make the approach and it was Walter Crickmer who met with James Gibson to formalise the agreement. Some sources claim Louis Rocca, the Chief Scout at Manchester United, made the connection with James Gibson. This is not true - Louis Rocca knew many people in football, but he was not the man who brought James Gibson to Old Trafford. Although these events have become somewhat confused over a period of time, records are very clear as to how James Gibson used his skills and qualities to resolve the hazardous situation Manchester United had found itself in.

To begin with James Gibson assessed the most recent balance sheet issued by the board of directors at the time. He examined this document with Mr Lawton, the chairman, and found that the Club had excess assets over liabilities of £38,000. On the face of things everything looked alright but James Gibson realised that the value of the land and buildings (estimated value £64,000) was included in these figures. On further inspection James Gibson concluded that the land and buildings were not worth anything like the estimated value - all of this meant that United was in debt to the minimum value of £26,000.

James Gibson also established that in the month he had agreed to take charge, the Club would lose an estimated £1965:00. The breakdown was as follows:

Income

Gate Receipts (3 league games)	£735:00
Central League Match	£30:00
Share of one away match	£130:00
Share of Cup Tie	£750:00
TOTAL	£1,645:00

Expenditure

Players & Staff Wages	£1,000:00
Players' Bonus	£100:00
Petty Cash Expenses	£250:00
Sundry trading accounts	£290:00
Hanson benefit/Interest	£665:00
Steward Benefit	£100:00
Rates & Tax	£200:00
Bank Overdraft Excess of Guarantee	£1,005:00 (*)
TOTAL	£3,610:00

Even though James Gibson was a shrewd and experienced business man with money to back the Club, he realised that he wasn't going to turn United's fortunes around in a short space of time. However, he was very clear with his objectives which were to hire a manager at £1000:00 a year and spend £12,000 - £20,000 on new players. But in order to achieve his aims James Gibson knew he had to have the support of the people in Manchester. On Tuesday 22 December he made the following comment in The Manchester Guardian:

"Though I have decided to see the United through the coming month, [says Mr Gibson] I am not prepared to be a `Milch Cow'." [In his opinion] "Unnacountable inertia is responsible for United's downfall. I do not blame the public for staying away from Old Trafford. The board of management has never taken the public into their confidence and they could not expect them to keep on rolling up at Old Trafford while a `hush hush' policy was being adhered to. I am at the head of United now and if the public will back me up and give me any justification for carrying on, I will assure them that the United will not fail. Manchester is surrounded with large towns to support two first-class teams. It will be some time before anyone can establish a winning team, and I do not intend to try immediately." (3)

(*) James Gibson later agreed to stand guarantor to the bank to the value of £40,000. By doing this he saved United over £1,000 per month and accepted the full risk for the Club.

James Gibson takes control

James Gibson's strong words did meet with some resistance from Mr Lawton and the board of management. For a while both the Manchester Guardian and the Manchester Evening News played the two chiefs off against each other. However, within a matter of days James Gibson assumed full control at United even though official appointments and resignations were not announced until January 20 1932. Assertive leadership tactics had won the day and provided the Club with a necessary kick. At a time of a national depression and high unemployment the fortunes at United were turning, and by providing this `lifeline' gift supporters had reason for optimism and real hope.

With the Christmas matches looming, James Gibson was given the green light by both the FA and the Club to choose the teams. The responsibility created an interesting dilemma. Since the Club had no manager, James Gibson could only turn to Walter Crickmer and the board of management for advice. But if he only did this how would the fee-paying public react, especially if matches were lost? Knowing that he didn't have the knowledge or the experience to pick a team on his own, James Gibson made a shrewd decision and first sought guidance from Mr Greenhough, the secretary of Manchester United's supporters' Club. Mr Greenhough commented on his own role in the Manchester Evening News (4).

"I gave Mr Gibson the supporters' point of view and Mr Gibson said that he would be pleased to have the supporters with him if he took over the Club permanently." He also went onto say, "That for the moment he could be well served by Mr Crickmer, Mr Jack Pullar (the trainer) and by Navigator." At that same meeting the subject of appointing a new manager was also discussed and James Gibson made it clear as to how he felt a successful Club needed to be run. Mr Greenhough added: "Mr Gibson told me that he would be looking for the sort of manager to whom he would give full control, and allow to reorganise the Club,".

This hands-off philosophy not only attracted Mr Scott Duncan in 1932, but more significantly drew a young Matt Busby to Manchester United fourteen years later at the end of the war.

James Gibson's message to supporters through Mr Greenhough and the press now needed a response. It came at his first game (Christmas Day 1931) when thousands of fans voted with their feet and by doing so handed James Gibson the only present he was asking for. Sources differ once again as to the exact number of people who watched United beat Wolverhampton Wanderers 3-2 (WW went onto win division 2), but it was a famous victory witnessed by more than 15,000 people than had paid to see the previous home game against Bristol City. However, the following day reality struck. In the return match at Molineux, Wolverhampton Wanderers beat United 7-0.

Plans for the future

The New Year saw James Gibson take full control of the Club and all the directors apart from the secretary, Walter Crickmer, resigned from the board. A letter of approval arrived from Mr C E Sutcliffe, Vice President of the League, wishing the Club every success and James Gibson set about rebuilding United. Pledging extended support he drew up a three year plan which was publicised in the local papers (5). The plan stated:

1. Mr Gibson will give an undertaking to the Club that he will take over the whole of the liabilities, subject to the first and second mortgages agreeing to withhold demand for payment of principal for two years unless the assets of the Club are placed in jeopardy.

2. Mr Gibson to have the option of repaying the mortgages within two years.

3. On the present board of directors retiring, Mr Gibson will undertake to form a board of directors acceptable to the shareholders.

4. Mr Gibson is prepared to send a letter to the present directors of the Club embodying these terms, but subject to his appeal for £20,000 being successful.

5. The proceeds of the appeal for £20,000 are to be put into a separate account at the National Provincial Bank Limited, Spring Gardens, Manchester in trust and earmarked "Solely for Transfer fees".

The mortgage holders voted unanimously to accept the conditions, and by doing so backed James Gibson. However, his appeal to supporters for a trust fund for players met with limited success, and by the time he took over the Club officially on January 20 1932 there was only £100:00 in the fund. This included a postal order for one shilling from a man who claimed he couldn't make it to Old Trafford on Saturdays, but hoped that his offering could keep United together. Although no records are available to prove where the extra money came from, it is believed that James Gibson used his own money once again to help the Club buy new players.

The other four directors who joined James Gibson on the new-look board of management included: Colonel Westcott, a former Lord Mayor of Manchester; Mr Hugh Shaw, a cotton-mill director at Stalybridge; Mr Matthew Newton, a director of Horrockses Crewdson Ltd in Manchester and Councillor A Thompson.

By the end of the 1931/32 season United had finished in twelfth position in Division 2. A lot of money was spent on new players and included Moody, a goalkeeper and Black, a centre-forward.

At the time of the take-over, talk had been of certain relegation, but the loyalty and efforts of the Manchester people had ensured a remarkable turn-around. After being defeated by Tottenham on January 23, United only lost three further games during the whole of the season.

The closed season

Manchester United 1932-1933

Old Trafford became a hive of industry during the closed season in 1932. Renovation and modernisation of the ground and stands created a new air at the Club and the mood of optimism suggested that United could be challenging for promotion the following year.

Mr Adam Scott Mattheson Duncan also arrived at Manchester United on Wednesday July 13 after agreeing a five year contract deal to manage the Club. A former Glasgow Rangers, Newcastle United and Scottish International footballer, Scott Duncan had experienced success at the top level. His reputation as a team-builder went before him. Prior to his signing with United he had spent eight years nurturing a great team at Cowdenbeath, many of the players under his wing becoming stars in their own right. The Manchester Evening News (6) told readers how Scott Duncan wanted to build a team.

"The principle upon which I will work at Old Trafford", he said "is to make football stars rather than buy them. I would rather build soundly and well, creating a good all-round average rather than have an unbalanced side with two of the greatest football stars in the country.

"I would like immediately to tell the Club's supporters that they are the people I am depending upon as much as anyone to bring First Division football back to Old Trafford. They must give every ounce of encouragement of the proper sort to the players."

James Gibson had invested hard. His courage, determination and belief that the people of Manchester deserved two football teams was paying off. United had marched purposefully away from an abyss that had threatened to swallow them forever. Now with a new manager, a renovated ground, a fresh strip for the team and confidence within the Club, United appeared ready to advance and challenge for promotion.

The following cartoons, all drawn by George Butterworth, tell the story of the home games during the 1932-33 season.

1932-33 Season

Preparing for their first match of the 1932-33 season, Manchester United are ready to "boot away" the all-fault-finding critics, with aspirations of returning once again to the First Division, from which they had been relegated in 1931.

Despite losing the first game of the season to Stoke, the undertakers will have to wait a while before they nail United into a coffin, having been revived by a 1-0 away win against Charlton Athletic.

Having been given a 4-2 caning by Southampton away from home, an angry supporter tells United not to go to the seaside again!

Six games into the season, Manchester United have notched up only four points thanks to an away win, a home draw with Charlton and a 1-1 draw with Grimsby. Nevertheless, this record compares favourably with the rather unimpressive 2 points gained by United's "brother", Manchester City, at the same stage in the season.

Nine games into the season, the United engine is yet to get going. Whilst the forwards have netted only 10 goals, the defence has let 17 slip through.

A new kit brings a change of fortune for United and as they prepare to play Bradford, they do so having beaten Burnley 3-2 away from home the week before.

By the 5th of November 1932, Manchester United, it seemed, were set for a good bonfire night, and as they prepare to put Notts County on the fire with a home win, they can already glow with pride after three very encouraging results. Indeed, United's key firework, Reid, had managed to score the 2 goals which sunk Bradford (2-1 win) and three out of the seven goals scored against Millwall (7-1 win) in two consecutive matches. Reid now resolves to score five goals in one match, which is music to the Directors' ears.

Gee Bee pokes fun at the refereeing which saw Frame's departure from the field at the game against Port Vale.

Invasion of the Scots! New manager Scott Duncan is impressed by the footballing talents to be found in the Highlands, and decides to recruit a number of players for United.

The cartoon says it all. Manchester United's faithful dream of triumphs and glories over the Christmas period against Lincoln, Swansea, Plymouth and Stoke.

Having beaten Plymouth 3-2 on Boxing Day, Scott Duncan now prepares his team as best he can for the important Third Round Cup Tie against Middlesbrough on the 14th of January.

New Year Tidings come from Gee Bee in the form of a stern reminder of past misfortunes, in the hope that United's players, especially the new recruits, will not give supporters deja-vous, and instead will lead them on the road to Wembley.

It's the FA Cup Third Round and optimistic suggestions are made for United's use of the Cup, once they have brought it home! But they face a stiff tie against Middlesbrough.

Despite losing 4-1 to Middlesbrough in the Cup, changes at Directorate level bring strengthened focus on the forthcoming fixtures and the need for United to fight for a good league position.

Manchester United's bid for the top of the table will mean some fierce encounters with the other leading teams which include Bradford, Nottingham Forest, Bury and Swansea. This new wave of optimism follows a recent 2-1 victory against Spurs.

Four matches undefeated, United's Scottish team members are proving worthwhile investments as they move closer towards the top of the table.

Despite beating Burnley 2-1 in the last home game, United's promotion dreams hit a brick wall when they are beaten 2-0 away at Millwall.

By all accounts, Manchester United had been on top against Notts County, another arch competitor in the promotion stakes. The 1-0 defeat did not reflect the balance of play - nevertheless, goals win games!

United are likened to the defeated Oxford Boat Race crew, "resting on their oars", as a result of their 3-1 defeat by Fulham.

This is reference to the new Season tickets on sale, now payable in instalments. James Gibson, President, sees this cash-flow exercise as the solution to financial shortcomings from which the Club still suffers.

The announcement of the opportunity to buy tickets in advance draws supporters in their hoards to Old Trafford's Ticket Office, no doubt to the delight of Club Secretary, Walter Crickmer.

Finishing in 6th position, Manchester United will remain in the Second Division, but thanks are given to the efforts of Messrs Gibson and Duncan, whilst the supporters are "awarded medals" for their support throughout the season.

Great Expectations

United managed to finish sixth in the second Division in the 1932/33 season, six places higher than in the previous year. However, they had only scored 43 points, one more point than in 1931/32, and throughout the season there had been much criticism of the forward line. The team was constantly reminded by the press of its weak front-line and even after the first game at home against Stoke which United lost 2-0, there was pressure on Scott Duncan to make immediate amends.

The initial pledge made by Scott Duncan in July 1932 that he wanted to make good players rather than buy them already had a touch of naivety about it. His confident nature and buoyant style had been greeted warmly by the people of Manchester when he arrived, but it seems that expectations were raised too high too quickly. Scott Duncan brought invaluable experience and knowledge of the game, but before coming to Old Trafford the new manager had never seen any of the team play. He did not know the inherent strengths and weaknesses at the Club and he hadn't been through the turmoil during the Christmas of 1931.

Poor results created frustration and unease which undoubtedly led the board to sanction the buying of new players. Along with the director, Mr Thomson, Scott Duncan travelled back to his homeland where he signed Frame (Cowdenbeath) and later Chalmers (Heart of Midlothian). Frame was a spirited 24 year old who was rated to be one of the finest centre half-back players in Scotland. Chalmers was an inside forward who had gained Scottish honours and was looking to play in the bigger English league.

Frame and Chalmers played their first game together for United against Preston North End on October 1 in front of a crowd of 20,000 people. Although the game was scoreless the press were more keen to report the importance of buying such good players rather than dwell on the disappointing result.

" United's supporters should feel gratified at the efforts which the controllers of United are making to re-introduce football of quality to Old Trafford. The present Manchester United Board are among the most earnest and wholehearted in the country. They did not wrap up the needs of their side, but admitted they were many, and set about trying to solve them in a manner which gave further evidence of their earnestness.

"With the coming of these two men from Scotland, however, the team building is only just beginning." (7)

The paper's report was proved right. Throughout the season Scott Duncan went in search of and bought new players such as George Vose (signed professional forms), Neil Dewar from Third Lanark, W Stewart from Cowdenbeath and E. W. Hine from Huddersfield. He continuously worked at building a team that blended well and produced the right results - but his efforts were not rewarded with any silver. By the end of the 1932/23 season United were still in the second Division. However, reminded by James Gibson's pledge in 1931 that it would take a long time to turn United's fortunes around, the people of Manchester remained patient and optimistic and looked forward to the new season.

Perhaps 1933/34 would be the year. James Gibson had promised and provided ground improvements, a quality manager, new players and financial stability. Support for United had grown tremendously, helped partly by one of James Gibson's bright initiatives. He had asked the Great Central and North Staffordshire Railway Committee if it were possible for trains to stop at the Old Trafford station next to the ground. An agreement was reached and at a cost of £140:00, platform steps were built and the siding and loading dock were removed. Fans no longer had to walk miles to watch United play. The highest attendance that season was 35,000 when United defeated Millwall 7-1 on October 22.

Unfortunately, James Gibson's second full season in charge at the Club proved to be one of the worst on record. Defeat followed defeat and pressure mounted on United from all quarters. Both Colonel Westcott and Councillor Thompson resigned from the board and James Gibson almost withdrew the financial support which was holding the Club together.

"He [James Gibson] was no longer prepared to guarantee the bank overdraft, now standing at £17,705 (of which the widow of J.H. Davies, however, was responsible for a guarantee of £5,000). After discussion he retracted, and agreed to continue his aid as before, subject to the Club `giving him a charge over its assets'. (8)

The newspapers were highly critical of the amount of money spent on players (approximately £20,000) but also demanded further changes in the team. Scott Duncan bought and sold ferociously in an attempt to stem the tide and avoid relegation to the anonymity of the third division. In total a record 38 players were used in the season and only five of the team that played in the first game against Plymouth Argyle played in the famous match away to Millwall on May 5 1934. It was the last match of the season and United had to win to stay up. And win they did. Manley and Cape scored the goals in the 2-0 victory and the team returned to Manchester as heroes.

The next season United again just failed to win promotion, finishing 5th. But in 1935/36 they became Second Division champions playing 19 consecutive matches without defeat. The following cartoons from Geebee's collection depict the two seasons leading up to United's winning of the league.

1935-36 Season

James Gibson had arranged for the trains to stop at Old Trafford, in the hope of drawing crowds through easier travel access. This is the first cartoon of the 1935-36 season. Manchester United, still in the Second Division, have ambitions for Promotion and the Championship.

Having lost the first match of the season 3-1 away at Plymouth, Manchester United have since pulled a 3-0 win over Charlton out of their bag of tricks, leaving match day opposition, Bradford City, wondering what else United might have up their sleeves.

Goal merchants, United, recently defeated Newcastle 2-0, bringing their scoring tally to nine in only five games.

"Big Chief United" plays the tom-tom triumphantly after a convincing 2-0 victory against Hull City. So far, United are having a "roaring" start to the season!

In this battle between home-towns, Manchester City were "cracked" at home by Stoke City, whilst Manchester United "shattered" Port Vale away from home.

Having let only 3 goals through in the last 9 games, United's defence is proving fairly watertight, whilst Manager, Scott Duncan, needs to give his forward-line more attention.

United's position is looking good after 12 games, but there's still a lot of work to be done if the team is to reach that Utopia called "Promotion". Leicester City wait in the wings to clip off United's tail.

Three consecutive defeats, and only one goal having been scored in those, turns United's prior good run into reverse gear. The supporters feel that the weakness is in the forward-line to the extent that a medicinal boost is perhaps the only cure!

United find flying form once again with a 5-3 win against the Canaries (Norwich City), with strikers Manley and Rowley netting 2 and 3 goals respectively.

Similar to a Gee Bee cartoon produced back in the 1932-33 season when United were beaten by Southampton "at the seaside", this cartoon depicts the 4-1 thrashing United had just received from Blackpool, also away from home.

Boxing Day Venue: a rather timid Barnsley awaits its "Christmas Box", in the knowledge that United have given Nottingham Forest a 5-0 drumming in the last game.

Half way through the Christmas fixtures, United face a daunting list of hard matches including a Cup Tie and League Games against Newcastle and Bradford in the New Year.

Having beaten their opponents, the two Manchester teams rejoice together, as they move into the next round of the FA Cup. United won 3-1 against Reading on the 11th of January.

Having defeated Reading, United had to play Stoke City in the next round of the FA Cup. United held on to a 0-0 draw away from home, and now they prepare, hopefully erosion-proof, for the replay at Old Trafford.

United's Cup dreams are dashed by Stoke City who won 2-0 in the replay, but Mancunians instead rally around their other home-town club, Manchester City, who are still in the race.

A recent good run in League matches gives United a good chance of promotion to the First Division. Sixteen games remain, the last fixture being held on 2nd May at Hull City's ground.

This cartoon would suggest that Manchester "beat" Sheffield United 1-1 in their recent clash, and that despite the equal allocation of a point each, United deserve more points so as to catch up the Division's leading teams West Ham, Spurs and Charlton.

Unbeaten in the last seven games, United's last victims were West Ham who suffered a 2-1 defeat much to the distress of top teams Charlton Athletic and Sheffield United.

Ten games to go and United are having fun at the Coconut Shy, knocking off some of their remaining opposition in order to win promotion.

In a tight 2-2 draw against Fulham, United's impressive run of being undefeated in ten consecutive games could have come to an end but for the heroics and acrobatics of John Griffiths on the day.

Well placed in the League Table, United have five more matches to play. However, they cannot afford to lose, and must seek to gain as many of the 10 points available if they are to achieve promotion.

Facing bury in the last home game of the season, United battle it out for the top slot in the Division with Charlton Athletic and West Ham.

As it transpired, United achieved their dream of promotion to the First Division. Undefeated in the League since 26th December 1935, United's New Year Resolution to finish top had been kept - and kept well!

The following cartoons depict football at Manchester United during the 1936/37 season

1936-37 Season

A brand new season and a welcomed return to the First Division, United face top-class teams, whom they must "overtake" or even "run-over" on their journey to the top of the table.

Manchester United's initiation test is proving difficult; having lost the last two, albeit very close, games, the squad realises that the First Division clubs know all the tricks of the trade, and swift adaptation will be the key to survival.

The long awaited derby! The city of Manchester buzzes at the prospect of the forthcoming clash between "brothers" - United and City.

Proud Mancunia' gives United its support (having won the derby 3-2) as it prepares to do battle with the mighty teams of Preston, Sheffield Wednesday and Arsenal.

Biblical connotations as United, against all odds, hope to slay the Goliath of the First Division - Arsenal.

Ironically, United had beaten "impregnable" Arsenal 2-0, but immediately suffered 4-0 and 2-1 defeats by Brentford and Portsmouth away from home. Returning to Old Trafford, they face another daunting opponent in the form of Chelsea F.C.

Three out of the last four matches have been lost and Manchester United are near the bottom of the First Division. Dramatically, Arsenal too is falling down the League ladder.

Scott Duncan, Manager, is having difficulties with his forward line and must rectify what has been a drought in United's scoring and winning abilities.

United's "illness" has been worsened by Liverpool, Grimsby and Leeds United, but Manager Scott Duncan optimistically determines to give his team fresh stamina.

A poor league run forces the club to concentrate on their forthcoming FA Cup Tie with Reading, in the hope that this competition holds more fortune for a struggling United side.

Christmas 1936 holds little more in store for United than a plethora of stiff league matches.

Having beaten Bolton Wanderers twice over the Christmas period, much needed points are collected and a renewed United look to shrug off their poor season results to date, and instead resolve to improve their position in the New Year.

The return match against Derby County brings back memories of the September '36 fixture, where Derby had the fortune to beat United 5-4. This time round, Manchester pray for that extra bit of luck.

It's FA Cup Day for United - they face Reading in the Third Round. Moreover they have tough league matches shortly afterwards against Preston and Sheffield Wednesday to look forward to!

Bruised and bandaged from a recent Sheffield Wednesday League defeat and Arsenal Cup-Tie 5-0 thrashing, the United side is asked to find the same valour and courage they displayed against the self same Arsenal earlier in the season, and repeat the winning score-line in the forthcoming clash.

Drawing 1-1 away at Arsenal, Manager Scott Duncan is confident that United are finally getting over the "League Wall" away from the ladder of relegation into the Second Division.

United face Portsmouth defiantly, despite recent Cup and League defeats by Arsenal and Brentford.

No chinks were made in Portsmouth's armour, which allows the threat of relegation to rear its ugly head once again.

A rather tired and apathetic United have failed to catch vital league points, having lost 3-0 to Charlton the week before. Moreover, they now face Grimsby who seem to be steaming along quite happily!

The United supporters have remained faithful to their team throughout this turbulent return to First Division football. Nourishment is required in the form of wind against the Merseyside duo - Liverpool and Everton.

Still hanging onto its confidence, Manchester United are trying to scare relegation away, aided by two convincing wins against the "Toffees" (Everton).

It's the last home game of the season. United are soon to be under fire from Middlesbrough, West Brom and Sunderland, and the second Division hole is too close for comfort. As it turned out, Manchester United finished 21st and were forced back into the clutches of the Second Division.

Highs & Lows

By winning the Second Division Championship in 1936, United had demonstrated a miraculous turn-around of fortune. The sceptics had been silenced and the patient optimists had been duly rewarded. Frank Carruthers writing in the Daily Mail on May 4 of that year compared the successes of United and Charlton, two sides that had won through against all odds.

"It is a happy reflection of the season which has just ended that outstanding success has come to two clubs who three or four years ago were in peril of going under and who were rescued by nothing less than grand sporting philanthropy.

"The public of Manchester owe it to Mr J.W. Gibson that there will again be first-class football at Old Trafford next season. Mr Gibson shouldering all the burden of Manchester United, has been responsible for as much as £25,000." (9)

But surviving the first division proved too much for United. The team was immediately relegated after one year in the top flight, finishing 21st and winning only ten games all season.

Again, the media clamoured for better players to bolster the forward line. Wingers were very much in fashion and many believed United should invest in players famous for their dazzling displays on the touch-line. But another philosophy was brewing at Old Trafford at the time.

James Gibson had said from the outset that he wanted to develop young talents and build from within. Walter Crickmer, the Company Secretary and Tom Curry (Trainer) were also of this belief. This idea was the foundation for the Manchester United Junior Athletic Club (MUJAC) and one of its first beneficiaries was a sprightly Charlie Mitton who was later to become one of United's most famous players.

Charlie joined the groundstaff in 1936 as a 15 year-old. The wages were £2:50 per week but from this he had to pay his digs which cost £1:50. The young boy had been recruited locally and was brought to the Club by Scot Duncan who had been impressed with ability whilst watching him play for a lesser known side. Charlie found the manager easy to get on with and from the outset struck up a good working relationship.

Before playing in the `A' team, Charlie worked in offices directly below those occupied by `management'. Whilst filing papers and completing menial administrative tasks he recalls that he often heard James Gibson and Scott Duncan expressing loudly their differences of opinion. The Chairman and the manager wanted results for the Club and for it to stay in the First Division. However, they often found it difficult to agree as to which players to buy and what should be paid for them.

Eventually things came to a head in November 1937. United were again struggling for form in the second division when suddenly the Manchester papers announced that Scott Duncan had decided to leave Old Trafford.

"At a full meeting held at the ground at Old Trafford last night, Manchester United Football Club directors acceded to Mr A. Scott Duncan's (their manager) request and released him from his agreement with the Club. Mr Duncan has been invited to manage Ipswich Town a non-league Club. His contract with Manchester United had still three and a half years to run." (10)

In fact the newspapers made relatively little of Scott Duncan's decision to leave, suggesting that United were keeping tight-lipped about the affair. The match programme that appeared on 20 November said that; "The Directors will be grateful if the supporters will disregard all rumours, published or otherwise, relative to the vacancy in the post of manager of the Club. The matter is one receiving the careful and continuous consideration of the Board, and the many friends of the Club will be officially informed through this programme in due course, as and when a decision is arrived at."

What is known however, is that just prior to Scott Duncan's departure, the directors had sanctioned the spending of £17,000 on new players because performances had been so poor. But on October 4 Scott Duncan told the newspapers that he was unable to buy players because he had had forty transfer bids refused.

"Clubs that could be attracted by offers of £2,000 or £3,000 for a player two years ago will not even look at such an offer today. We have got the money to buy players and we want to strengthen our team, but as matters stand at the moment the position with regard to transfers is almost impossible. The trouble is this. Clubs that were not doing too well two or three years ago are now receiving better gates and they have realised the way to wipe out a bank overdraft is by means of the turnstile receipts." (11)

In other words, it had become a sellers market. Scott Duncan felt he had to have more money to buy the players he wanted, but no-one knew how much he needed. Whilst some directors became increasingly uneasy, James Gibson decided it was time to take action.

For some while James Gibson and his family had taken to spending holidays in Bournemouth at their second home, Tudor Cottage on Overcliffe Drive. His son, Alan Gibson, recalls that his father regularly went off to watch the town's football team play. After one particular match in October news broke that John Rowley, Bournemouth's prolific outside left, had been signed to United for £3,000.

Rowley was a strong and skilful 19 year old who was considered to be Bournemouth's best player. Charles Bell, Bournemouth's manager at the time was distraught and told the Manchester Evening News. "They have taken my best player from me. There was not another player in the team to touch Rowley, who has not missed a match since he came to us." (12) The loss of Rowley was then compounded only a few days later, when another Bournemouth forward, Stan Pearson, also agreed terms with United.

Both players were to become two of United's pre-war heroes, scoring many of the goals that took the Club back into the First Division in 1938. However, Scott Duncan's credibility and integrity had been undermined by James Gibson. Players had been signed by someone other than the person who best understood the team. The Chairman's impulsive behaviour was the final nail in the coffin and a few weeks later Scott Duncan resigned.

For the rest of the 1937/38 season the Club was managed by the ever-present Walter Crickmer, who oversaw the team's promotion back to the First Division. A grateful and jubilant James Gibson again talked about the development of the Junior Athletic Club. "On 3 May the Chairman emphasised the necessity for a pitch for practice games and for the `A' team, and stated that he had been making enquiries about a tenancy of the old Broughton Rangers Rugby Ground. By 21 June this tenancy was secured." (13)

The MUJAC flourished helped by a committee of local teachers and coaches from Manchester University. By 1939 the junior team had won the Chorlton Amateur League scoring a total of 223 goals. The Chairman emphasised that United did not own the young players. `We only tell them that we hope that if as a result of what the Club has done they rise to anything like fame they will bear the Club in mind.' James Gibson now had his vision laid out in front of him - to develop a team of young Manchester players who could one day play for United.

But unfortunately, War in Europe was developing and the MUJAC scheme had to be put on hold. Even so, the seeds had been sewn and when the conflict was over everyone knew that the Club could resume with the idea and make it work. This new-found confidence in the Junior Club was helped by United's standing in the First Division. By finishing 14th in the league they had reached their highest position for ten years.

Picer and Pegler's summary report on Manchester United issued just before the War.

James Gibson's accountants, 'Picer and Pegler', of Fenchurch Street in London summarised the Club's position just before the war.

Mr. Gibson is the Chairman and also the pre-denominating influence in this Company. He has guaranteed the overdraft of the Company with the National Provincial Bank. Which on the 28th May, 1940, stood at about £22,000, and which will probably continue to increase throughout the War.

There is a first mortgage on the property and on the floating assets of the Company for £25,000. Mr Gibson has a second mortgage which can be called upon by him in respect of any payments made under his guarantee.

The latest accounts available are those for the year ended the 13th May, 1939. These show a profit of £5,993. The issued capital is £5,229, and the balance to the credit of profit and loss account at the 13th May, 1939, was nearly £50,000.

The ground is situated at Trafford, and a very large sum of money has been spent on improving it and on erecting stands which will now accommodate, I am told, about 80,000 persons. The land, buildings, and stands, appear in the Balance Sheets 1939 at over at over £77,000. I was informed by Mr. Gibson and by M. Halliday, the Manager of the National Provincial Bank, that the land covered by the property measures 47,476 square yards. In addition to the stands and other accommodation, there are two houses. I was told that adjoining land has sold for 25/- to 30/- per square yard. On these figures the land is worth about £60,000 apart from the stands and equipment. The land is freehold with the exception of a small portion which is held on a 999 year lease.

The second most important asset shown in the Balance Sheet is "Players Account". This stands at over £38,000 and represents the cost price of players adjusted by the profit and loss on the sales of players.

In present conditions the value of this asset is more than doubtful as many players have joined up for active service and may unfortunately never return.

There is no other asset of any value.

Football is practically at a standstill and will be so until the end of the war. Meanwhile, certain expenditure on upkeep has to met and it is because of this that the overdraft will increase. A few games are been played and a small revenue is being earned, but it is unlikely that this will cover the necessary expenditure.

It is understood that the site has now been let as a Government store, from which an income of £3,000 or more a year may be obtained.

Mr. Gibson's position in this matter is somewhat difficult. He is regarded in Manchester as the man who saved the Manchester United Football Club, and he has undoubtedly done a fine piece of work for this Club. Given normal circumstances the position would no doubt right itself in time, but there will be difficult times ahead, and Mr. Gibson has to face a substantial liability on this account.

While it is true that if the Manchester people want to keep the Club going they should come to its assistance, it is highly unlikely that any big effort to save it would be made at the present time, and Mr. Gibson's alternatives to-day appear to be either to carry the burden or to try to dispose of the ground, stands and equipment. Unless it can be used for War purposes, a sale seems to be likely.

The following cartoons depict football at Manchester United during the 1937/38 season.

1937 - 1938

Finding themselves once again in the Second Division, Manchester United prepare for battle! Their first match of the season will be at Old Trafford against Newcastle United, who in the 1936-37 season has the distinction of winning more matches away from home than any other club in the second Division.

Three games into the season, "valiant" United have beaten mighty Newcastle, but have fallen foul of Coventry City and Luton Town. Both matches were lost 1-0 away from home, leaving manager Scott Duncan looking for a sharper forward line.

Like boxing, football's all about points! A revitalised United were clearly on top - but at the end of the day, the score-card showed a 2-2 draw, which was not a fair reflection of the balance of play.

This cartoon refers to the 1-0 defeat by Stockport County on the 18th of September. However, it is perhaps slightly unfair, as the forward line notched up six goals in the two matches prior to Stockport consequently giving Manchester two much needed wins.

There's no doubt that so far the season is proving turbulent. The United team seem to run into streaks of good, and then almost inevitably bad, form. This rather depressing cartoon refers to the recent defeat by Southampton.

A hint of optimism from the United faithful as their team brings back a triumphant three points from Tottenham.

The critics still have time to suggest that United are not making any progress in their quest for First Division promotion, but this picture illustrates how other leading second division clubs are struggling in the extreme to scale the heights United have climbed to in the League table.

A complete turn-around of fortune! Previously carrying the weight of gloom on its shoulders, United have turned the tables, having scored seven goals against Chesterfield in the last match.

'COME TO THE FAIR'

In the space of four matches, United have dramatically shot up the League table, and a win against Swansea on the 4th of December will take them even closer the Leadership position

A KICK IN OUR PANT-O SEASON!

Four consecutive thrilling victories against Chesterfield (7-1), Aston Villa (3-1), Norwich City (3-2), and Swansea (5-1) come to a painful end when Bradford issued a reminder that it's not all plain sailing to the top. That reminder was a harsh 4-0 defeat!

The 1937 Christmas fixtures brought good cheer to United's league position and a plump stocking brimming with points. Two consecutive victories against Nottingham Forest, and a draw against Newcastle United, give supporters fresh aspirations for promotion and Cup Glory.

Whilst United wait to travel further towards Wembley, having quickly sent Yeovil Town packing with a convincing 3-0 FA Cup Third Round win, the team relishes the prospect of a battle with Luton Town - especially when it's wearing its untarnished magic league football boots!

A fierce FA Cup Forth Round Tie with Barnsley away from home had resulted in 2-2 draw. Now, United challenge Barnsley in the replay on Old Trafford's familiar turf.

A 2-1 Win against Sheffield United away from home gives Manchester another three points, and it certainly seems as though the First Division is the likely destination for Mr Gibson's players.

This is a reminder to supporters, critics and forthcoming opponents that United are a formidable side and that the ominous FA Cup Fifth Round show-down with mighty Brentford shall be fought fiercely and in the same spirit which has brought success so far.

FA Fifth Round defeat means that United should now concentrate on league promotion. Quite inexplicably, however, the team throws away valuable points unnecessarily, to an otherwise weak Tottenham Hotspurs eleven.

This match against Blackburn Rovers is to be the third consecutive game played at Old Trafford. United have recovered from their 1-0 Spurs defeat, picking up three points from a 4-0 solid victory over West Ham United.

The "trophies" on the walls at Old Trafford serve to scare match-day opponents Fulham into defeat before the ball is even kicked. An impressive list of victories against the division's other leading promotion contenders, allows United to be confident against the likes of Fulham.

It's a race to the finish and United are well placed to take promotion. But to do so will mean an encounter with Aston Villa, who are also battling for a place in the First Division.

Despite a 3-0 defeat by Villa, fortune aids United in its promotion race and the team still has a chance of finishing in one of the top two league positions.

By no means making it easy for themselves, Manchester United have picked up only two points from their last three matches, and they need wins if possible from their remaining games.

Three games left. United need to obtain as many of the nine points available to them as they can, if they are to join Aston Villa in the First Division next season.

Aston Villa, who have already secured promotion, is "electing" his queen. That throne must go to either Manchester United, Coventry City or Sheffield United.

Facing Bury in the last game of the season, Manchester United completed a triumphant 2-0 victory and rightfully claimed the "seat" next to Villa. Eighty-two goals had been scored in a season which comprised twenty-two wins, nine draws and eleven losses. Mr Gibson can now look forward to his team's return to England's First Division.

Out Of The Ashes

A sorrowful Alan Gibson recalls the day when his father heard that Old Trafford had been bombed by the German Luftwaffe. It was the morning of March 12 1941. "He just broke down in the lounge at `Alanor' and wept" said Alan, "It was a tragic sight."

Old Trafford Bombed

That night-time destruction of the Stretford End Stand and the damage caused to the rest of Old Trafford caused much distress and anguish in the Gibson household. Ten years of work had been ruined, or so it seemed to the Chairman of the Club - a dream had been shattered and a great friend lost.

The accountant's report made just before the outbreak of war in 1939 had strongly hinted that James Gibson might sell the Club. But who would pay a fair price for Manchester United now? The buildings and stands were almost worthless and there would be a high cost for clearing the derelict site. And what about income from matches? Although the Club did not have the same overheads for players there were still high maintenance fees and costs for administering matches in the newly devised regional leagues.

Fortunately, directors on the board at Manchester City made a quick and generous decision and proposed that Maine Road be used as a temporary home for United. The offer was immediately accepted by James Gibson and for eight years both Clubs shared the same ground. Without that kind and spirited gesture United would never have managed to win the Football League North Region (1942) and play in the final of the North Cup (1945). More significantly, the name of Manchester United would never have been on the FA Cup trophy in 1948.

Throughout the rest of the war United attempted in vain to persuade the Government to help finance the redevelopment of the ground. And in fact it wasn't until November 1944 when the War Damage Commission granted a license of £4,800 for the demolition of the grandstand that any progress at Old Trafford was made at all. But much greater financial assistance was needed if Old Trafford was to be restored to anything like its former glory. Although James Gibson could not put forward further money his business dealings had put him in touch with someone who was prepared to help.

Prior to the war starting, James Gibson had expanded his clothing business and had moved the main factory to Enderley Mills in Stoke-on-Trent. Whether it was providence or fortune, he came into contact with Mr Ellis Smith, the local MP and by chance a keen United supporter. Ellis Smith knew about the bombing of Old Trafford and having met with the Chairman agreed to fight for the Club's cause in the House of Commons.

In November 1947 in the House, he asked the Minister of Works how many First Division Clubs that had suffered damage from air-raids had been rebuilt. This exacting query immediately gave the issue a much needed political profile and it was to be the catalyst for much further debate and deliberation. In total, ten clubs including Manchester United were found to be in need of financial support.

But although the Government appeared sympathetic towards the cause, postponement and set-backs followed - whilst there was a will in Manchester to re-create the splendour of Old Trafford the way was blocked. It seemed the Government would not provide funds for a rebuilding programme The Manchester Evening News captured the mood of frustration in January 1948.

"Further efforts are to be made to persuade the Ministry of Works to allow Manchester United's stands to be built from scrap materials. Qualified engineers and welders are prepared to do the work in their spare time, and the Ministry has been told that there is plenty of unused steel scaffolding available.

"A deputation recently saw the Minister of Works, Mr Charles Key, in an effort to persuade him to grant a license for the materials required. This was followed by a personal plea by Mr Ellis Smith who today received a letter from Mr Key saying that his department is restricted by the conditions for issuing licences imposed by the White Paper on capital investments, which limits the work on sports grounds to that required for the removal of danger to the public." (14)

Walter Crickmer seemed resigned to the fact that a licence would never be granted. But Ellis Smith viewed matters differently and only a couple of months later his perseverance made him the hero of Manchester. On March 15 1948 the Government gave the green light for the repairing of the bomb-damaged ground. In total the Club was granted £17,478, more than £12,000 than any other of the nine clubs receiving financial support.

However, the board of directors realised that this sum was not enough to rebuild the main stand and although they were extremely grateful for the efforts made by Ellis Smith, felt disappointed that more money was not forthcoming. Walter Crickmer, secretary, continued to liaise with Ellis Smith who in turn maintained pressure on the Minister responsible for ground repairs. Although it took a further two years for anything to happen the Government did eventually grant a further licence of £25,000 for the building of a new stand.

Matt Busby
A New Manager at United

It is not inconceivable that United's improved performances and success in the League and FA Cup leading up to March 1948, had affected the Government's decision to grant a licence.

Since the football league had resumed in 1946 United had twice finished second behind Liverpool and Arsenal respectively. The team that won national admiration with the media contained many familiar faces - Johnny Carey, Jack Rowley and Stan Pearson had survived the ravages of war and returned eager for football at United. In addition, United were able to draw on the services of youngsters that had been part of the Junior team before the war. Charlie Mitten for one was a player of immense talent who for some years would make the inside-left position his own.

And the man who called the tune and blended these players together was Matt Busby. At 34 Matt was still a comparatively young man but his experience at Manchester City and Liverpool had provided him with a valuable insight into the methods of management and the psychology of players both as individuals and as a team. He had learnt as a footballer that if he ever became a manager he must work very closely with a team in order to fully understand abilities, gain respect and bring the best out of all. Furthermore, when it came to the board of directors, he knew that he could not live under a cloud of fear and obligation. Matt Busby was single-minded and was prepared to be his own man, and this was his message when he first visited James Gibson to discuss terms in February 1945.

Matt Busby was working as a PE instructor in Italy when he received a letter from Louis Rocca informing him of the vacancy. The opportunity struck a chord with Matt. Both he and his wife, Jean, liked the people of Manchester and the new position provided the kind of challenge that appealed to his nature.

Since Old Trafford was still unusable in 1945 James Gibson and Matt Busby met to discuss matters at the Coldstorage buildings, 2 miles from the ground next to the Manchester Canal. The meeting was frank and Matt Busby made it clear that he had been made other offers by clubs such as Liverpool. However, he said that his preference lay with United and James Gibson thanked him for his `honesty of purpose'. An historic agreement was made that day and on February 15 the directors met to confirm the arrangements. On February 19 the papers sang out the news that United had captured a great footballing name.

"Company Sergeant-Major Instructor Matt Busby, Liverpool right-half back and Scotland captain today signed an agreement to become manager of Manchester United when he is demobilised. Only a few years ago Busby, (now 34) who has proved himself one of the greatest halfbacks of modern times was the `forgotten' man of international football.'

Attractive Player

His thousands of Manchester fans remembering him as a stylish and attractive player when he turned out for Manchester City unswervingly believed in his brilliance when Scottish selectors seemed to have neglected and forgotten him.

And he justified their faith. After one pre-war international cap in 1934 he was ignored until the 1941-42 season, since when he has appeared for Scotland in 8 games, several times as Skipper."

Although he didn't know it, James Gibson's had made an inspired choice and had paved the way for over twenty years of glorious footballing success at Manchester. Back in 1931 when he had been first appointed Chairman, James Gibson had said that he `wanted to appoint a manager `whom he would give full control, and allow to reorganise the Club'. (4)

Matt Busby grabbed control of the team with both hands and began to mould them into the sort of outfit that he knew would win matches. Jimmy Delaney, a right wing, was one of the very few purchases he made although it is widely believed that James Gibson paid for this rising football star out of his own pocket. However, rather than spend money on lots of new players the new manager wanted to use the resources that the Club possessed. In 1960 Percy Young wrote: "What Busby did (and has done consistently), was to make the players aware of their own capabilities, and those of their colleagues. He experimented positionally until he discovered the effective combination." (15)

However, Matt Busby's single-minded approach didn't always meet with James Gibson's approval and more than once the two men argued over the development of the team. Sandy Busby, Matt Busby's son, agreed that after the war James Gibson always wanted his father to buy new players whenever they appeared on the market.

One day James Gibson became so angry because his manager wasn't prepared to purchase new players. He waved his stick at Matt Busby and ordered him to go out and buy or else. But Matt Busby was resolute - he knew exactly the shape of the team he was building and he said that he would not be bullied into a decision. James Gibson left the room and returned a short while later to apologise for his actions and accepted that it was the manager's job to choose the team. That day James Gibson gave away control and by doing so provided Matt Busby with the reins to create and build teams that could win trophies. The Chairman's autocratic style had been vital during the ten-year rescue of the Club. He had won many friends and doubtless made a few enemies. But now at the age of 69 he wasn't a young man; he also had to change his approach so that the Club could progress even further.

By establishing common ground on this issue the two men developed tremendous mutual respect for each other. James Gibson allowed Matt Busby the freedom to develop the teams so long as he brought success to the Club. And success came rapidly. Between 1946 and 1952 United won the Championship (51/52), were runners-up on four occasions and won the FA Cup in 1948.

That FA Cup victory is still believed to be one of the best ever, United winning 4-2 against Blackpool. On their way to the cup, United defeated Aston Villa (6-4), Liverpool (3-0), Charlton Athletic (2-0), Preston North End (4-1) and in the semi-finals Derby County (3-0) - in this match Stan Pearson scored a brilliant hat-trick. By winning the Cup Manchester United secured their position as one of if not the most feared teams in the League and the following year (August 24 1949) the Club celebrated its much awaited return to Old Trafford

It had taken nearly eighteen years, two managers, a hat-full of players and a bombed stadium for the Club to find itself back at the top of football. Throughout, United had depended on James Gibson's unswerving commitment and love for the Club and his honest approach to all the people with which he had dealings.

Sadly, not long before the victorious FA Cup final James Gibson suffered a stroke and was unable to attend the match. However, when the team returned to Manchester, the open top bus went straight to James's house so that the players could meet their Chairman and present the trophy to him. It was an emotional return but a fitting one for a man who had promised the people of Manchester success at United.

For over three years James Gibson's illness continued. His son Alan and great nephew, Alan Embling, both remember his stubborn fight against ill health and his determination not to beaten by it. But following another damaging stroke in September 1951, James Gibson passed away.

In that year Manchester United won the Football League and the rest is history. James Gibson's generosity and dedication must always be remembered.

James Gibson. Taken from the original oil painting.
E.H. MOONEY 1932

A Tribute To George Butterworth

All the cartoons that appear in this book were drawn by George Butterworth.

Born on 5 January 1905 in Wordsmoor near Stockport in Cheshire, George developed an early interest for caricatures. He first studied at Stockport College and went on to the Manchester School of Art where he learnt quickly from others and cultivated his very fine illustrative skills.

After completing his formal education, George first found work with the Stockport Advertiser. In 1923 he went on to work as a full-time artist with the Kemsley Newspaper in Manchester and it was here that he became a sports cartoonist and created the name 'Geebee'. This pen-name can be found on all the cartoons in this book.

Inevitably, George Butterworth's sports cartoons attracted the attention of James Gibson. Impressed by the detail and life-like caricatures, the Chairman commissioned cartoons for each match programme - the dedication and imagination of the cartoonist are self evident in the pictures. His unique style and understanding of life at United earned him universal respect.

When war broke out George Butterworth turned his attention to political cartoons. He worked for several papers including: the Empire News, Daily Dispatch, Sunday Chronicle and News Chronicle before finally moving to the Daily Mail. Right through to his retirement in 1968 he continued to create entertaining and highly original pieces of work.

His wife, Betty Bidwell, said that life with George was tremendous. Although the job as a cartoonist was often strenuous, he was always able to see the funny side of things.

George Butterworth
By courtesy of Mrs. Betty Bidwell.

This book is sold subject to the conditions that it shall not, by way of trade or otherwise, be lent, resold, hired out or otherwise circulated without the publisher's prior consent in any form of binding or cover other than that in which it is published and without a similar condition including this condition being imposed on the subsequent purchaser.

© Questions Answered 1994

The Gibson Guarantee by Peter Harrington

Published and Printed by Imago Publishing

Design and Typography by PDP

ISBN 0 9515972 4 8   £12.99